With love to our little angel, Zach
~ Mimi

THE WISE ANIMAL HANDBOOK

Kate B. Jerome

ARCADIA KIDS

Attempt new skills from time to time.

Just try to think them through.

And if you find you're left behind...

...then change your point of view.

Try not to think of just yourself.

Invent new ways to share.

Stay close to friends whom you can trust.

But
always
be
aware.

Avoid the tattle in the tale.

Insist that truth is best.

Embrace with pride
the strengths you have.

Demand
to be
impressed.

Enjoy the peace that nature brings.

Ignore what's just for show.

Join forces when the road gets rough.

Admit when you don't know.

Remember **family** is the best.

Despite the ups and downs.

Don't **hide** from things that you must **face.**

Make
joyful
laughing
sounds.

Eat healthy food to grow up strong.

Be patient with your friends.

Try not to take a stubborn stand.

Be **quick** to make **amends.**

Excuse yourself when manners slip.

Be helpful every day.

Keep trying even when it's hard.

But don't forget to play!

And sing

... and dance each day!

Written by Kate B. Jerome
Design and Production: Lumina Datamatics, Inc.
Coloring Illustrations: Tom Pounders
Research: Eric Nyquist

Cover Images: See back cover

Interior Images: 002 Anetapics/Shutterstock.com; 003 George Green/Shutterstock.com; 004 Sergey Uryadnikov/Shutterstock.com; 005 Gnomeandi/Shutterstock.com; 006 Bruce MacQueen/Shutterstock.com; 007 Henk Bentlage/Shutterstock.com; 008 M.M./Shutterstock.com; 009 Mikael Damkier/Shutterstock.com; 010 Brendan van Son/Shutterstock.com; 011 Michael Pettigrew/Shutterstock.com; 012 StevenRussellSmithPhotos/Shutterstock.com; 013 Pakhnyushchy/Shutterstock.com; 014 Patjo/Shutterstock.com; 015 Quinn Martin/Shutterstock.com; 016 Lincoln Rogers/Shutterstock.com; 017 Dirk Ercken/Shutterstock.com; 018 Karel Gallas/Shutterstock.com; 019 Orangecrush/Shutterstock.com; 020 Guenter-foto/Shutterstock.com; 021 Janecat/Shutterstock.com; 022 Shironina/Shutterstock.com; 023 Annette Shaff/Shutterstock.com; 024 Vitaly Titov/Shutterstock.com; 025 Rohappy/Shutterstock.com; 026 MattiaATH/Shutterstock.com; 027 Otsphoto/Shutterstock.com; 028 FikMik/Shutterstock.com; 029 Four Oaks/Shutterstock.com; 030 Ekaterina Kolomeets/Shutterstock.com; 031 Hugh Lansdown/Shutterstock.com.

Published by Arcadia Kids, a division of Arcadia Publishing and The History Press, Charleston, SC

For all general information contact Arcadia Publishing at:
Telephone: 843-853-2070
Email: sales@arcadiapublishing.com

For Customer Service and Orders:
Toll Free: 1-888-313-2665
Visit us on the Internet at www.arcadiapublishing.com

Library of Congress Cataloging-in-Publication data is on file with the publisher.

Printed in China

Bottlenose Dolphin

Read Together

The bottlenose dolphin lives underwater, but it can't stay there all the time. That's because this beautiful animal breathes air to stay alive—just like you!

Domestic Pig

Read Together

Why do pigs like to roll in the mud? They probably do it for a few different reasons. One reason is to stay cool. Another reason is to use the mud as sunscreen. Can you think of a third reason? *(Hint: why would YOU like to roll in the mud?!)*

Green Tree Frog

Read Together

There are many different kinds of tree frogs. The American green tree frog is found mostly in the southeastern United States. Males can inflate, or blow up, a sac under their mouth to make their calls much louder.

Chug Puppy

Read Together

What do you get when you cross a Chihuahua and a Pug? A cute little Chug puppy! Did you know a dog's nose print is one of a kind? It's like your fingerprint—which is special just to you!